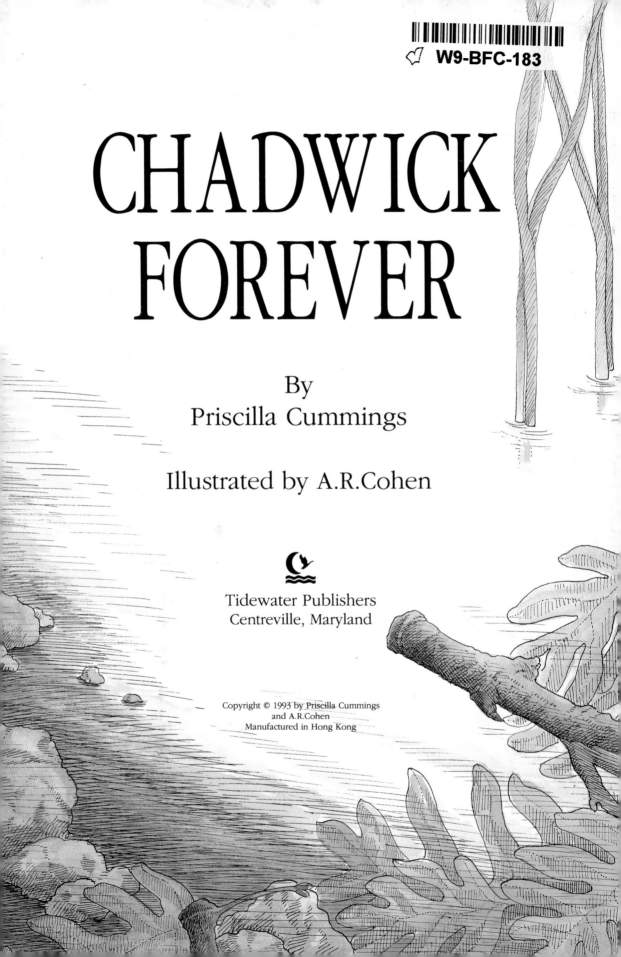

CHADWICK FOREVER

By
Priscilla Cummings

Illustrated by A.R.Cohen

Tidewater Publishers
Centreville, Maryland

W ho's crying?" Chadwick asked as he and Esmerelda peeked above the calm waters of Shady Creek and gazed toward shore.

Bernie the Sea Gull cocked his head to the wind. "Sounds like it's coming from that tree."

The crying grew louder and louder until all at once it stopped. From out of a dark hole halfway up an old oak, objects began flying into the air.

"What in the world is going on?" Bernie wondered aloud.

Esmerelda sighed. "I knew something would happen just when we were going to make our big announcement."

"That can wait," Chadwick said. "No one even knows we're back from our honeymoon yet."

Crackety crack! BOOM!! Branches snapped off the tree as still more objects fell to the ground.

Chadwick turned to Bernie. "You'd better fly in and take a look."

Cautiously, Bernie circled the tall oak several times, trying to peer in through the thick, leafy branches. He couldn't be sure, but he thought he saw a small rocking chair sail into the bushes far below.

Now, wait a minute, Bernie thought as he held out his wings and drifted in for a closer look. Wasn't this Hester's oak? Could it be that the tree's resident squirrel was just doing a bit of vigorous housecleaning? After all, Hester was known for her tidiness.

Just then, a large saucepan was hurled out of the hole. Bernie veered to one side as it whizzed past him and fell, clunking and clanking, through the limbs below.

"Hester! Watch out!" he squawked. "You nearly beaned me in the head with that pot!"

Although he didn't normally land in trees, Bernie settled onto a sturdy branch and, after ducking once more to avoid a flying footstool, picked his way over the tree's rough bark.

"Hester! Hold it!" he demanded.

Soft whimpering came from within the tree. Bernie paused, his anger melting at once into concern. "Hester, what's wrong?"

When there was no answer, Bernie peeked inside the front door to see the squirrel standing quietly, her eyes moist with tears. In her front paws she held a tray with an acorn tea set.

"Mother gave me these dishes," she sniffed. "It was a housewarming gift when I moved into this tree."

"I remember," Bernie said softly, his eyes opening wide at the sight of Hester's empty apartment. Only a straw rug remained, rolled up and propped against a set of empty shelves that had once been stacked neatly with bundles of dried flowers and tin cans filled with nuts and seeds.

"This is next to go," said Hester as she prepared to heave the tea set out the front door.

Bernie lifted his wings to stop her. "Now, wait a minute. What's going on here?"

"I'm leaving," Hester explained bitterly. "My kind won't
be around much longer. So I'm returning to my birthplace,
a loblolly pine at the refuge, to spend my remaining days. I
thought that at the very least I could throw my belongings
below for some needy field mouse."

Bernie didn't budge. And he didn't get it.

"What are you talking about? The last of your kind? There are a million squirrels like you running all over the place!"

Hester's eyes flashed. "There are a million *gray* squirrels all over the place!" she corrected him. "But there are not a million Delmarva Peninsula fox squirrels. That's part of the problem. No one knows the difference. And now *I* may be the only one left!"

"Who says?" Bernie demanded.

Hester put the tea set down and scooped up a large book from the floor. "See for yourself," she said.

Reluctantly, Bernie took the book and studied the title. He couldn't read very well and wished Chadwick were there to help him with the big words.

Hester grew impatient. "*Endangered Wildlife of the Chesapeake Bay*," she read aloud.

"Where'd you find this book?" Bernie asked.

"What's it matter where I found it? What's important is that it's about us poor creatures who may disappear forever—all because of something *man* has done." Snatching the book back, she flipped through the pages. "Page twenty-three. See? There I am. Delmarva fox squirrel."

It was Hester, all right. Funny, Bernie thought, but he had never noticed how different she was from the other squirrels. *Much* bigger—almost as big as a cat! Tail a tad bushier. Lots of white on the paws and tummy.

Hester waited, tapping her foot. "Well?"

"Golly, I don't know what all this means, but surely there's something we can do to help."

Hester shook her head and picked up the tea set again. "I don't think so. Animals can't fight back. What's done is done."

Bernie was firm. "At least talk to Chadwick."

Hester twitched her tail. "All right," she finally agreed. "But I'm telling you, it won't do any good."

At first, Chadwick was befuddled. He'd never heard of being "endangered" before and the whole idea overwhelmed him. He couldn't imagine a world without animals—or worse, a Bay without crabs!

He decided to call a meeting. Two notices went up immediately: one scratched on the sandbar, another posted behind the counter at Sid and Sal's Famous Channel Marker Diner.

Everyone had begun to gather when Bug-Eyed Benny shot through the water, screaming "Monster! Monster on the sandbar!"

The crabs zoomed down to deeper water and the birds scattered. In seconds, Shady Creek was deserted.

Still out of breath from the fast swim, the crabs resurfaced near a bell buoy out in the Bay. One by one, the birds showed up, too, some of them landing on the buoy and some floating nearby in the water.

"What kind of m-m-m-monster was it?" Pincher Pete asked.

Bug-Eyed Benny shook his head. "I can't describe it, Pete!"

Chadwick suspected the monster was nothing more than the little boy who came down to the creek now and then to tease the crabs by dropping smelly old chicken necks in the water.

"Was the monster wearing a baseball cap?" Chadwick asked.

Bug-Eyed Benny turned angrily. "It wasn't the boy," he snapped.

Chadwick remained calm. He knew Bug-Eyed Benny had a tendency to exaggerate. "Well. Was it a big monster or a little monster?"

Bug-Eyed Benny frowned and shrugged. "I don't know. I didn't see it."

Mouths, bills, and beaks dropped open. The animals began to suspect it was a false alarm.

"But I didn't make it up!" Bug-Eyed Benny exclaimed. "There really *was* a monster. I saw his tracks all over the sandbar! They were tracks like you've never seen before—long and squiggly and ugly! Whatever it was slithered right through the notice about our meeting!"

Just then, the buoy rocked to one side and its bell
made a loud clang.

"It's an omen," said Matilda as she struggled to keep
her balance on the buoy. "Those marks are a warning.
Something bad is about to happen."

Mrs. Mallard shuddered. "Matilda's right. Maybe we
shouldn't deal with this problem of endangered animals."

Several others nodded in agreement.

"Bunch of sissies," Chadwick mumbled. "Guess *I'll* have
to find out who messed up our sign!" Before anyone could
stop him, he slipped sideways beneath the surface and
swam off.

"Come back!" Esmerelda screamed.

In one lightning-quick move, Baron von Heron stretched out his long neck and plucked Chadwick out of the water. For the briefest moment, the crab dangled by one leg above the crowd before being daintily dropped back.

The Baron coughed and cleared his throat:

"One mustn't rush to be courageous
for causes that may be outrageous!"

Bernie flew to Chadwick's side. "The Baron's right," he said. "Don't do anything rash. We can't afford to lose *you!*"

Chadwick was disgusted. Nevertheless, he agreed not to try anything more.

Overnight, a high tide washed away the eerie tracks and the next day all the animals returned to Shady Creek. There was no more talk of bad omens or mysterious monsters. Chadwick rescheduled the meeting and everyone gathered at sunset.

Pleased with the turnout, Chadwick chuckled as he watched Hector Spector the Jellyfish blob this way and that, trying to decide on the best position.

"Don't forget," Matilda bent to whisper, "you and Esmerelda said you had something exciting to tell us, too."

Esmerelda beamed at Matilda and the two giggled.

"Later," Chadwick said firmly. "We need to talk about Hester's problem first."

Matilda straightened up and adjusted her glasses. "Hmmmph. If you ask me, Hester brought this whole mess on herself. She begs for trouble by going out in those fields every day. She ought to stick to trees like the other squirrels."

"But she's different," Bernie argued. "She showed me in a book. She's a Del . . . a Del-something squirrel. They get a lot of their food from fields. A big cornfield, a stash of soybeans—that's what she loves. But man keeps building houses in the fields and Hester has less and less to eat.

"Not only that," Bernie added, "but man is also cutting down the big trees that Hester likes to live in."

Matilda rolled her near-sighted eyes. "Well, I don't know why she can't stick to smaller trees and eat nuts, just because she's a Del-something squirrel!"

"Shhhhhh! Here she comes now," Chadwick said.

A hush fell over the group as Hester approached.
Quietly, she made her way down to the water's edge, where
she sat on her haunches and shook out her magnificent
tail. She wore a freshly pressed yellow apron and pulled
from one of its front pockets a small notebook.

"I hope you don't mind," she said without looking up.
"I'm keeping a journal of my last days."

Silence followed and all heads turned to Chadwick, who scratched behind his eye stalks with the tip of one claw.

"First things first, I guess. Is anyone else on this so-called endangered list? Don't be shy now," Chadwick urged.

"Indeed. Speak up! There is no shame!
It's man again. It's him we blame!"

The Baron had his say and then stepped back.
A flurry of bubbles announced that Belly Jeans the Flounder wished to speak. "My friend, Deke the fish, is on that list. He's a Maryland darter."

"The piping plover is on that list, too," said Oswald, the great blue heron, as he nodded toward the shy, gray bird at his feet. "She flew all the way in from the seashore for this meeting."

When the plover didn't speak, Oswald referred to his bird book. "It says here the piping plover likes to nest beneath the dunes, but that jeeps and trucks on the beach are scaring the little bird away!"

"That's right!" the little piping plover piped up. "I couldn't stay on my nest with all that traffic!"

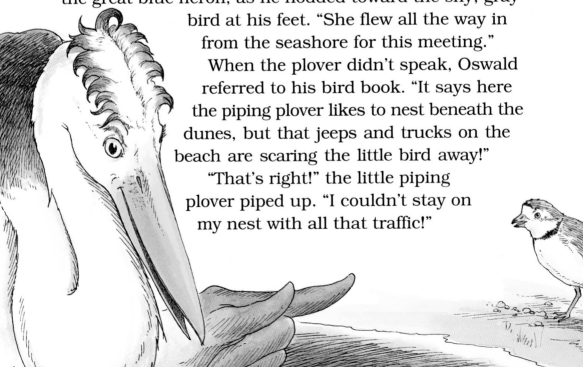

"Yes, indeed. The beach can be a dangerous place," agreed two beetles, who stood high on their long, dainty legs. "We're Puritan tiger beetles and we're endangered, too."

The tiger beetles were kind of cute, despite their fearsome name. When they spoke, their thin, sweet voices chimed in unison: "Can someone please help us?"

Just then, Lewis, an old turtle who had been living in Shady Creek for years, lumbered forward. Chadwick inched back, pulling Esmerelda with him. Chadwick had known Lewis to actually eat a crab or two when his appetite built up, and he wasn't about to become a snack for the old terrapin.

Bernie wasn't afraid, though. "You're not endangered, are you?" he asked.

"Not yet," Lewis answered in his deep, baritone voice. "But I may be soon. Did you know that forty-nine terrapins drowned last year after getting caught in a single crab pot?"

Lewis went on. "We're running out of sandy beaches, too, and we need sandy beaches to lay our eggs."

"So do we!" the tiger beetles exclaimed, surprised they had anything in common with a big old turtle like Lewis.

This was serious, Chadwick thought. Disappearing beaches, vanishing forests. He turned to Deke the Darter: "What's *your* problem?"

The little fish looked up, wide-eyed and innocent. "I just need clean water," he said.

It soon became obvious that the problem was widespread. Salamanders, woodpeckers, peregrine falcons—even a bald eagle showed up at the meeting—each had a different story to tell.

Things were getting complicated. Deep inside, Chadwick worried that there wasn't a thing any of them could do.

"We won't come to any conclusions tonight," Chadwick said. "So I suggest we continue this meeting another time. But before you leave, Sid and Sal have some refreshments."

"It's the least we could do!" Sal volunteered. "We ospreys were on that endangered list ourselves once!"

Spying the platters heaped with steaming seaweed cakes and swamp muffins, the crowd surged forward. Chadwick scuttled to the front, and held up both claws.

"Wait!" he shouted. "Esmerelda and I have something to announce first!"

Esmerelda blushed, then blurted out: "We're parents now! In early June I spawned my first mass of eggs!"

A cheer went up. Matilda was all aflutter with the good news. "I knew it! I knew it! How many? Oh, I do hope you named one for me!"

The question caught Esmerelda off guard. "How many?" she murmured to herself. "Why, I don't know exactly. About two million, I guess."

A loud gasp filled the air.

"Oh, my!" Matilda exclaimed, lifting a handkerchief to her bill.

For a moment, every creature on the sandbar envisioned a horde of little crabs overrunning the creek, bending the reeds, hiding in the marsh grass, stirring up the muddy bottom, eating everything in sight! Still, Chadwick and Esmerelda were very special and there was not a bird, beast, or fish among them who would not welcome the new family— however large it was.

Matilda clutched her hankie. "Well," she said shakily, "where *are* the little crabbie darlings?"

Chadwick and Esmerelda looked at each other and shrugged.

"We don't know exactly," Esmerelda said matter-of-factly. "Last time we saw them was a couple months ago, down at the mouth of the Bay." She smiled, remembering. "They were so beautiful, so perfect then. I hope they've hatched and molted into handsome jimmies and lovely little sooks by now."

"That's crab-talk for boys and girls," Bernie explained with a chuckle.

No one else was laughing, especially not mothers like Mrs. Mallard, who sat on her eggs for weeks.

"What?! You abandoned your babies?"

"You don't even know how many?!"

Bernie chuckled again. "You dummies. That's the way crabs do it. And don't worry. There won't be any two million *crabbie darlings* swimming up the creek! Most of 'em have probably already been eaten—slurped up by some gluttonous eel for dessert. Heck! Probably half of 'em got washed out to sea. Right, Chad?"

Chadwick nodded weakly and Esmerelda paled.

"Hey, I'm not saying some won't make it," Bernie added quickly. "Why, little Chadwick Junior is probably whipping those waves and riding that tide home to Shady Creek right now!"

"Yes. Yes, that's right," Chadwick hurriedly agreed, fearful that Esmerelda might faint. "We expect them soon— maybe even on tomorrow's first incoming tide."

No one knew quite what to say.

Hester put away her notebook and broke the silence. "Well, I think it's wonderful," she said. "We all do things differently. Congratulations, Chadwick and Esmerelda. I will never know your happiness, for I shall never have a handsome husband or a loving family. But you—and your little ones—why, you'll always know that some tiny bit of you, like the smallest star in the sky, shines on and on, for generations to come."

"Hey! I like that!" Bernie whooped. "Chadwick forever!"

"A toast to the new parents!" Dr. Mallard said, lifting a nutshell full of blackberry juice.

"Here! Here!" a heron called out as everyone showered the crabs with best wishes and plunged into the food.

No one noticed that Hester left without even taking a bite to eat.

*   *   *

During the night, a storm came through. The sound of raindrops hitting the oak's big leaves made me sad. It was almost as though the tree were crying for me. Oh, how I shall miss it here. Still, I have made up my mind to go.

With that, Hester closed her journal and placed it inside a bandanna with a small pile of acorns. At dawn, when the first dim fingers of light poked their way through the gray mist over Shady Creek, she set off on her journey to the refuge.

She was far away by the time the others woke up, and far, far away by the time the mysterious tracks were spotted again on the sandbar. She would never know just how much fear and worry spread through Shady Creek that day, not because there was an unknown monster lurking around, but because, in early afternoon, the animals discovered that Hester had left.

The first day is over. How exhausted I am. Have found a bed for the night in a wild cherry tree. I'm lonely without my friends nearby in the creek. Must try to sleep. Tomorrow I have to find a way across the river.

For a squirrel, the only way across the Tred Avon River was to sneak aboard the ferry that ran from Bellevue to Oxford. Hester and her mother had done it once many years ago. Now Hester would have to do it by herself.

All afternoon Hester watched from beneath a bush on the riverbank. When the ferry pulled into Bellevue, she picked up her bundle and held it close. She could feel her heart pounding.

Two cars and a truck waited in line for the ferry. When their engines started, Hester scampered unnoticed to the loading dock and hid behind a pile of rope.

One car rumbled onto the ferry, then the other rolled aboard and jerked to a stop. Hester peered over the edge of the dock at the dark river water swirling below. Her tail twitched rapidly. She knew it was time to make her move.

A rusty pickup truck rattled past.

Now! Hester told herself. But her legs froze.

Chains rattled. A man's voice called out orders. The vehicles were in place and the ferry's big propellers whirled, churning the water into a froth.

Chug-a-chug-a-chug-a-chug-a-chug. The ferry moved forward. Hester would have to leap across the water now if she wanted to get aboard.

"Don't do it!" a voice screeched from above.

Too late. Hester was in the air, reaching with her front paws for the edge of the ferry. She missed it by a hair.

As she plunged into the white, rushing water behind the ferry, Bernie squawked and circled above.

Finally, Hester bobbed to the surface, gasping for breath and paddling frantically with her tiny paws to keep afloat. Bernie's eyes darted around. He spied a large branch in the water and dove down to pull it her way.

Hester grabbed on.

"Don't let go!" Bernie shouted.

The strong, swift current carried the branch downriver. Already weak, Hester knew she couldn't hold on for very long.

Bernie swooped low to the water and tugged at the branch with his beak, coaxing it toward shore.

"Oh, help me," Hester moaned.

Luck was with them. The branch caught the edge of a fallen tree near the riverbank and stopped. Exhausted and drenched, Hester dragged herself ashore and collapsed in the brown mud.

Within moments, Dr. Mallard arrived, carrying his black medical bag under one wing. Hester was still unconscious. The doctor wrapped her in a blanket and two blue herons flew her home in a sling.

When I awoke, I was back in my own apartment, where all my furniture had been put back just the way I had it! There was even a pot of tea, warmed and waiting. And my journal, which Bernie found. My dear friends have taught me one thing: I'm going to stop worrying about tomorrow and enjoy the life I have today! This is where my heart is. I shall never leave Shady Creek again.

Hester closed her notebook just as Bernie stuck his head in the doorway.

"Hester, come quick. There's trouble on the sandbar. They've cornered the monster who's been leaving those ugly tracks."

"You don't say!" Hester exclaimed, snatching a shawl and scampering out the door.

A small crowd had gathered and Chadwick's voice could be heard. "Stop sniveling!" he ordered. "No one's going to hurt you! We just want to know who you are."

At first Hester thought Chadwick was talking to Orville Oyster. But when the mysterious shell spoke, its voice was high and smooth, like that of a young child.

"I'm a mussel," the shell said, "a dwarf wedge mussel. I don't mean anyone harm. And I'm sorry I messed up your sign with my tracks, but I heard about your meeting and I wanted to come. I'm endangered too, you see. The pollution is just killing me."

"A *dwarf wedge mussel?*" Bernie had to stifle a laugh. "You've got to be kidding."

"He's not kidding," said a rather deep and stirring voice from the back of the crowd. "Why would he joke about something as serious as who he is?" A large, stately squirrel in a top hat stood behind them on the sandbar.

"And who are you?" Bernie demanded.

"The name is Harrison," the squirrel said as he touched his hat with the tip of an elegant walking stick and bowed ever so slightly. "I'm looking for someone."

Hester peeked out from behind Baron von Heron, intrigued by the handsome stranger.

"Just who are you looking for?" Chadwick asked.

Harrison folded his white front paws on top of his walking stick. "I won't know until I find her," he said. "You see, I'm looking for a wife. But the search has been long and hard because there aren't many of my kind left in these parts."

"Your kind?" Matilda looked down her bill at the squirrel.

"I'm a Del—"

"A Delmarva fox squirrel?" Hester asked.

"Yes! That's it, my good woman! However did you know?"

Well. No one had to guess what was happening. It was love at the first twitch of their tails! Paw in paw, the two squirrels headed at once to Hester's tree for tea.

After they left, Chadwick went over to the tiny mussel and assured him he was welcome in Shady Creek. "I just can't promise you that things will get any better here," he said. "It's up to the people to stop building on our fields, cutting down trees, and ruining beaches. It's up to them to keep the water clean."

The mussel said he understood. "I guess we just have to hope that the people will help, right?"

Chadwick nodded and tried to smile.

Before long, night came again to Shady Creek and the animals dispersed, some returning underwater, some heading to the marsh. The soft glow of candlelight and the sound of gentle laughter came from Hester's oak apartment.

Only Chadwick and Esmerelda remained on the sandbar in the moonlight, watching as an incoming tide lapped at the sand around them.

They were happy for Hester, yet sad for the others whose future was unknown. They felt a little sorry for themselves, too, for they had hoped that on this night they would be reunited with their own little ones. Yet, in their hearts they knew—as all the animals knew—that this was the way of life. One day happiness, one day sorrow. Life went on regardless. Already Esmerelda was planning to spawn a new mass of eggs.

"It'll be all right. You'll see," Chadwick said, putting his claw around Esmerelda.

She frowned at him. "Shhhhh. I hear something."

Chadwick listened. A breeze rustled the nearby marsh grass, carrying with it bursts of faint, high-pitched sounds.

"Mummy! Mummy! Mummy! Daddy! Daddy! Daddy!"

Esmerelda turned to Chadwick. "The children!" she exclaimed. "The children are here! They're here!"

Sure enough, the little crabs had arrived, hungry and tired, with the tide.

With open claws, Chadwick and Esmerelda scooped up their new family while all the other birds and animals rushed back to the sandbar to see what all the commotion was about.

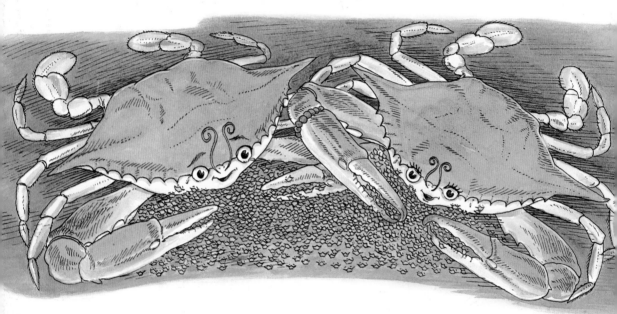

The piping plover piped a happy song. Esmerelda beamed proudly and Chadwick found he had to wipe away a tear of joy.

Hester couldn't wait to get back to her journal that night.

After all the baby crabs arrived, Harrison and I looked up into the night sky. Such a clear night. There must have been a million stars out! It made me feel warm inside to think that maybe there really was a tiny, bright light up there, shining forever, for each and every one of us.